What's Love?

Shelley Rotner
and Deborah Carlin

Photographs by Shelley Rotner

A NEAL PORTER BOOK
ROARING BROOK PRESS
NEW YORK

A Neal Porter Book
Published by Roaring Brook Press
Roaring Brook Press is a division of Holtzbrinck Publishing Holdings Limited Partnership
175 Fifth Avenue, New York, New York 10010
www.roaringbrookpress.com

Distributed in Canada by H. B. Fenn and Company Ltd.

Cataloging-in-Publication Data is on file at the Library of Congress
ISBN-13: 978-1-59643-362-5
ISBN-10: 1-59643-362-0

Roaring Brook Press books are available for special promotions and premiums.
For details contact: Director of Special Markets, Holtzbrinck Publishers.

First Edition January 2009
Designed by Hans Teensma, Impress, Inc.
Printed in China

1 3 5 7 9 10 8 6 4 2

Dedicated to the ones we love.

Love is as big as a harvest moon,

as wide as a summer sky.

Love opens our heart.
It makes us giggle and sometimes cry.

Love lets us share. Love helps us trust.

We love the animals that live with us,

and those that are wild and free.

We love the people in our life.
We love our families

and our friends.

We love our neighbors

and our teachers.

And we love ourselves.

We love the feel
of our bodies moving.

We love the art we make.

We love the music we play.

We love the buzz of ideas
and stories in our heads.

We love the colors and shapes
in the world around us.

Love brings us joy like the first spring flowers.
Love comforts us like a strong, old tree.

Love is a gift from me to you
and from you to me.

What do *you* love?